Pebble® Plus
Bilingüe/
Bilingual

Presidente/President
Barack
Obama

por/by Jennifer L. Marks

Editor Consultor/Consulting Editor:
Dra. Gail Saunders-Smith

Consultor/Consultant:
Dra. Andra Gillespie
Department of Political Science
Emory University, Atlanta, Georgia

CAPSTONE PRESS
a capstone imprint

Pebble Plus is published by Capstone Press,
151 Good Counsel Drive, P.O. Box 669, Mankato, Minnesota 56002.
www.capstonepress.com

092009
005618CGS10

Books published by Capstone Press are manufactured with paper containing at least 10 percent post-consumer waste.

Library of Congress Cataloging-in-Publication Data
Marks, Jennifer, 1979–
  [President Barack Obama. Spanish & English]
  Presidente Barack Obama / por Jennifer L. Marks = President Barack Obama / by Jennifer L. Marks.
  p. cm. — (Pebble Plus bilingüe/bilingual)
  Includes index.
  Summary: "Simple text and photographs describe the life of Barack Obama — in both English and Spanish" — Provided by publisher.
  ISBN 978-1-4296-4594-2 (library binding)
  1. Obama, Barack — Juvenile literature. 2. Presidents — United States — Biography — Juvenile literature.
I. Title. II. Title: President Barack Obama. III. Series.
E908.M3718 2010
973.932092 — dc22   2009030380

Editorial Credits
Erika L. Shores, editor; Strictly Spanish, translation services; Katy Kudela, bilingual editor; Veronica Bianchini, designer; Deirdre Barton, photo researcher; Eric Manske, production specialist

Photo Credits
AP Images, 11; Punahou Schools File, 13; Ron Lewis, 25; Seth Perlman, 17
Corbis/John Wrin/Harvard University, 15; Martin H. Simon, 19; Orjan F. Ellingvag/Dagbladet, 23; Reuters, 5, 7, 9
EMMANUEL DUNAND/AFP/Getty Images, cover
Getty Images/AFP/TIMOTHY A. CLARY, 27
Library of Congress, 29 (both)
Shutterstock/Alan Freed, 21; mistydawnphoto, 1
Wikipedia, public-domain image, 28 (both)

Note to Parents and Teachers

Presidente/President Barack Obama supports national history standards related to people and culture. The images support early readers in understanding the text. The repetition of words and phrases helps early readers learn new words. This book also introduces early readers to subject-specific vocabulary words, which are defined in the Glossary section. Early readers may need assistance to read some words and to use the Table of Contents, Glossary, Internet Sites, and Index sections of the book.

Table of Contents

Tabla de contenidos

Student of the World

Barack Obama was born in Honolulu, Hawaii, on August 4, 1961. His mother, Ann Dunham, was from a small town in Kansas. His father, Barack Obama Sr., was from Kenya.

Estudiante del mundo

Barack Obama nació en Honolulu, Hawai, el 4 de agosto de 1961. Su madre, Ann Dunham, era de un pequeño pueblo de Kansas. Su padre, Barack Obama Sr., era de Kenya.

born in Honolulu, Hawaii/nació en Honolulu, Hawai

1961

Young Barack in Hawaii, date of photo unknown/
Barack de niño en Hawai; se desconoce la fecha
de la foto

Education was important to Barack's parents. When Barack was 2, his father left to go to Harvard University. Barack stayed in Hawaii with his mother and her parents.

La educación era importante para los padres de Barack. Cuando Barack tenía 2 años, su padre se fue a estudiar a Harvard University. Barack se quedó en Hawai con su madre y los padres de su mamá.

born in Honolulu, Hawaii/nació en Honolulu, Hawai

1961

Barack saw his father again in 1971./
Barack vio a su padre otra vez en 1971.

In 1967, Barack and his mother moved to Jakarta, Indonesia. They lived with Lolo, Ann's new husband. Barack saw many poor people in Jakarta. Their struggles made him sad.

En 1967, Barack y su madre se mudaron a Jakarta, Indonesia. Ellos vivían con Lolo, el nuevo esposo de Ann. Barack vio mucha gente pobre en Jakarta. Sus problemas lo entristecían.

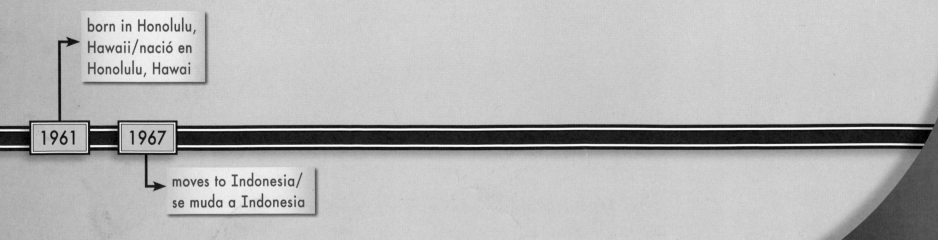

born in Honolulu, Hawaii/nació en Honolulu, Hawai

1961

1967

moves to Indonesia/ se muda a Indonesia

Barack with his stepfather, his mother, and half sister Maya in 1968/Barack con su padrastro, su madre y su hermanastra Maya en 1968

Ann wanted the best for her son. Barack could go to a better school in Hawaii. Barack returned there to live with his grandparents. He went to Punahou School in Honolulu.

Ann quería lo mejor para su hijo. Barack podría asistir a una mejor escuela en Hawai. Barack volvió allí para vivir con sus abuelos. Él asistió a Punahou School en Honolulu.

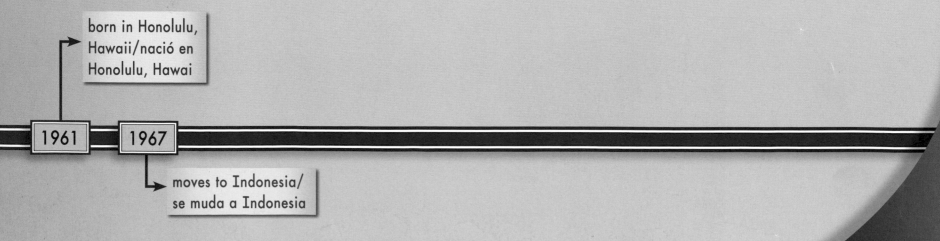

born in Honolulu, Hawaii/nació en Honolulu, Hawai

1961   1967

moves to Indonesia/ se muda a Indonesia

Barack with his grandparents at his high school graduation in 1979/Barack con sus abuelos en su graduación de la secundaria en 1979

Adult Life

Barack was a popular student and a good basketball player. After high school, he went to college. He graduated from Columbia University in 1983. Then he moved to Chicago. He worked to find people jobs.

Su vida adulta

Barack era un estudiante popular y un buen jugador de basquetbol. Después de la secundaria, él fue a la universidad. Se graduó de Columbia University en 1983. Luego se mudó a Chicago. Él trabajaba para encontrar trabajo a otras personas.

born in Honolulu, Hawaii/nació en Honolulu, Hawai

graduates from Columbia University/ se gradúa de Columbia University

1961   1967   1983

moves to Indonesia/ se muda a Indonesia

Barack with his high school basketball team in 1977/
Barack con su equipo de basquetbol de la secundaria
en 1977

In 1988, Barack left Chicago to go to Harvard Law School. He moved back to Chicago when he finished. In 1992, he married a lawyer named Michelle Robinson.

En 1988, Barack dejó Chicago para ir a Harvard Law School. Él se mudó nuevamente a Chicago cuando terminó. En 1992, se casó con una abogada llamada Michelle Robinson.

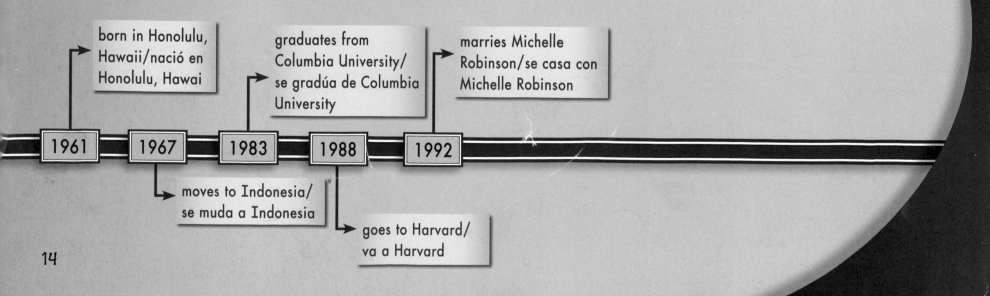

born in Honolulu, Hawaii/nació en Honolulu, Hawai

graduates from Columbia University/ se gradúa de Columbia University

marries Michelle Robinson/se casa con Michelle Robinson

1961   1967   1983   1988   1992

moves to Indonesia/ se muda a Indonesia

goes to Harvard/ va a Harvard

Making a Difference

Barack was elected to the Illinois state senate in 1996. He wanted to improve the state's schools. He wanted equal rights for all people.

Marca una diferencia

Barack fue elegido al senado del estado de Illinois en 1996. Él quería mejorar las escuelas del estado. Él quería igualdad de derechos para todas las personas.

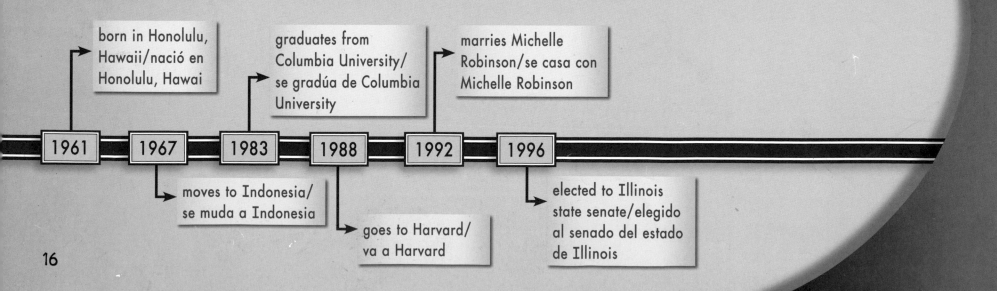

born in Honolulu, Hawaii/nació en Honolulu, Hawai

graduates from Columbia University/ se gradúa de Columbia University

marries Michelle Robinson/se casa con Michelle Robinson

| 1961 | 1967 | 1983 | 1988 | 1992 | 1996 |

moves to Indonesia/ se muda a Indonesia

goes to Harvard/ va a Harvard

elected to Illinois state senate/elegido al senado del estado de Illinois

16

While he served in the Illinois senate, Barack's daughters Malia and Sasha were born. In 2004, Barack became a U.S. senator. He wanted to help make people's lives better. In 2007, he decided to run for president.

Durante su servicio en el senado de Illinois, nacieron las hijas Malia y Sasha de Barack. En 2004, Barack se convirtió en un senador de EE.UU. Él quería mejorar la vida de las personas. En 2007, decidió postularse para presidente.

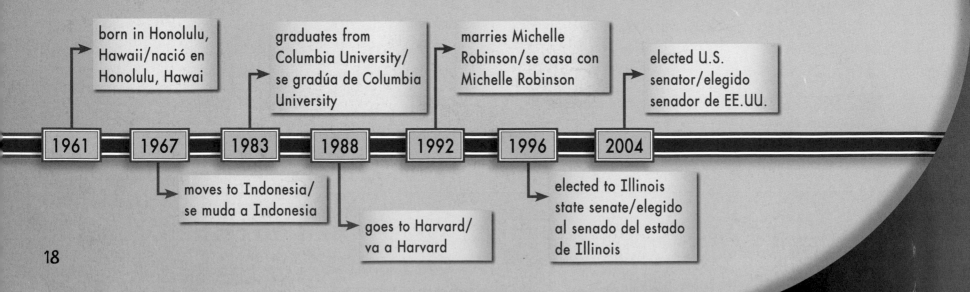

born in Honolulu, Hawaii/nació en Honolulu, Hawai

graduates from Columbia University/ se gradúa de Columbia University

marries Michelle Robinson/se casa con Michelle Robinson

elected U.S. senator/elegido senador de EE.UU.

| 1961 | 1967 | 1983 | 1988 | 1992 | 1996 | 2004 |

moves to Indonesia/ se muda a Indonesia

goes to Harvard/ va a Harvard

elected to Illinois state senate/elegido al senado del estado de Illinois

Barack gave speeches all over the country. He spoke about jobs, improving health care, and ending the Iraq war. His words gave people hope. Americans voted on November 4, 2008.

Barack dio discursos por todo el país. Él habló acerca de trabajos, mejorar la atención de la salud y terminar la guerra de Irak. Sus palabras dieron esperanza a la gente. Los estadounidenses votaron el 4 de noviembre de 2008.

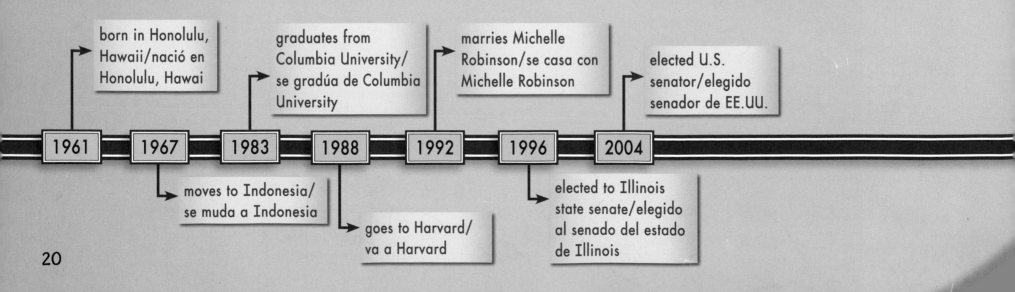

born in Honolulu, Hawaii/nació en Honolulu, Hawai

graduates from Columbia University/ se gradúa de Columbia University

marries Michelle Robinson/se casa con Michelle Robinson

elected U.S. senator/elegido senador de EE.UU.

1961   1967   1983   1988   1992   1996   2004

moves to Indonesia/ se muda a Indonesia

goes to Harvard/ va a Harvard

elected to Illinois state senate/elegido al senado del estado de Illinois

Winning the Election

By the end of the night, Barack had won enough votes. In Chicago, he gave an acceptance speech. The excited crowd cheered. Many were moved to tears. They shouted, "Yes, we can!"

Gana las elecciones

Al final de la noche, Barack había ganado los votos suficientes. En Chicago, dio su discurso de aceptación. La multitud alegre festejó. Muchos se emocionaron hasta las lágrimas. Ellos gritaron, "¡Sí, podemos!"

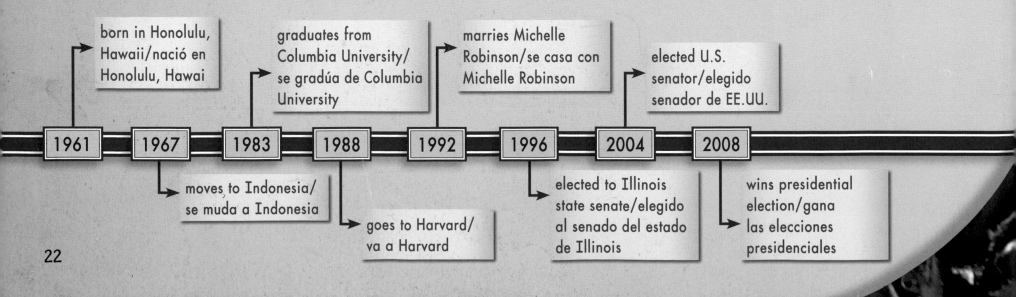

| 1961 | 1967 | 1983 | 1988 | 1992 | 1996 | 2004 | 2008 |

born in Honolulu, Hawaii/nació en Honolulu, Hawai

graduates from Columbia University/ se gradúa de Columbia University

marries Michelle Robinson/se casa con Michelle Robinson

elected U.S. senator/elegido senador de EE.UU.

moves to Indonesia/ se muda a Indonesia

goes to Harvard/ va a Harvard

elected to Illinois state senate/elegido al senado del estado de Illinois

wins presidential election/gana las elecciones presidenciales

The election made history. Barack was the first black president of the United States. Americans hoped Barack would bring even more changes to the country.

Las elecciones hicieron historia. Barack fue el primer presidente negro de Estados Unidos. Los estadounidenses tenían la esperanza que Barack traería más cambios al país.

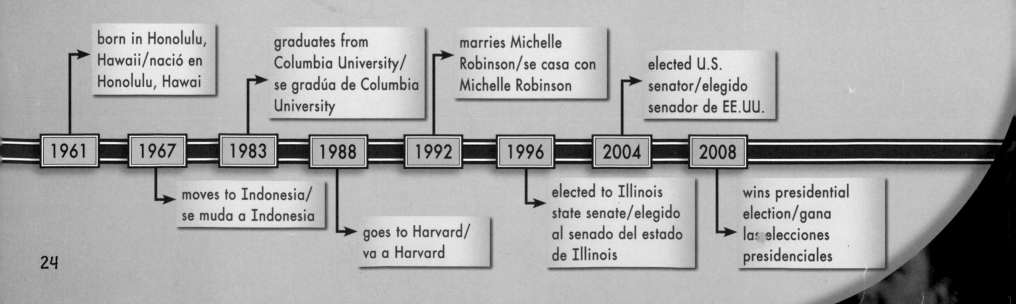

born in Honolulu, Hawaii/nació en Honolulu, Hawai

graduates from Columbia University/ se gradúa de Columbia University

marries Michelle Robinson/se casa con Michelle Robinson

elected U.S. senator/elegido senador de EE.UU.

1961 1967 1983 1988 1992 1996 2004 2008

moves to Indonesia/ se muda a Indonesia

goes to Harvard/ va a Harvard

elected to Illinois state senate/elegido al senado del estado de Illinois

wins presidential election/gana las elecciones presidenciales

President Obama

Barack Obama became the 44th U.S. president on January 20, 2009. Leading the nation wouldn't be easy. President Obama was ready for the challenge.

Presidente Obama

Barack Obama se convirtió en el 44º presidente de EE.UU. el 20 de enero de 2009. Dirigir la nación no sería fácil. El Presidente Obama estaba listo para el desafío.

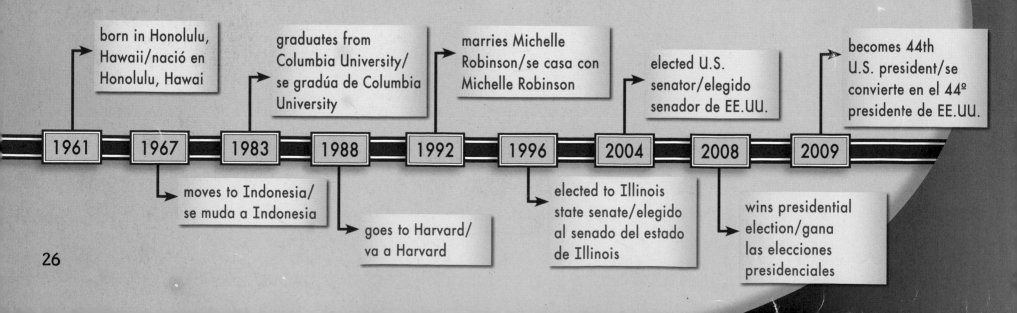

born in Honolulu, Hawaii/nació en Honolulu, Hawai

graduates from Columbia University/ se gradúa de Columbia University

marries Michelle Robinson/se casa con Michelle Robinson

elected U.S. senator/elegido senador de EE.UU.

becomes 44th U.S. president/se convierte en el 44º presidente de EE.UU.

1961 **1967** **1983** **1988** **1992** **1996** **2004** **2008** **2009**

moves to Indonesia/ se muda a Indonesia

goes to Harvard/ va a Harvard

elected to Illinois state senate/elegido al senado del estado de Illinois

wins presidential election/gana las elecciones presidenciales

Facts about / Datos sobre Barack Obama

Born/Nacimiento:
August 4, 1961/4 de agosto de 1961

Parents/Padres:
Ann Dunham and Barack Obama Sr./
Ann Durham y Barack Obama Sr.

Wife/Esposa:
Michelle Robinson Obama

Children/Hijas:
Malia, born in 1998; Natasha, or Sasha
for short, born in 2001/Malia, nacida en 1998;
Natasha o Sasha en forma abreviada,
nacida en 2001

Favorite book/Libro favorito:
Song of Solomon by Toni Morrison/*La canción de Salomón* por Toni Morrison

Favorite movies/Películas favoritas:
"Godfather I & II"/"El Padrino I & II"

Favorite sport/Deporte favorito:
basketball/basquetbol

Heroes/Héroes:
Martin Luther King Jr., Mohandas Gandhi,
Pablo Picasso, and **John Coltrane**

Hobbies:
spending time with Malia and Sasha,
basketball, and writing/pasar tiempo con
Malia y Sasha, basquetbol y escribir

Presidents of the United States / Presidentes de Estados Unidos

George Washington, 1789–1797
John Adams, 1797–1801
Thomas Jefferson, 1801–1809
James Madison, 1809–1817
James Monroe, 1817–1825
John Quincy Adams, 1825–1829
Andrew Jackson, 1829–1837
Martin Van Buren, 1837–1841
William Henry Harrison, 1841
John Tyler, 1841–1845
James K. Polk, 1845–1849
Zachary Taylor, 1849–1850
Millard Fillmore, 1850–1853
Franklin Pierce, 1853–1857
James Buchanan, 1857–1861
Abraham Lincoln, 1861–1865
Andrew Johnson, 1865–1869
Ulysses S. Grant, 1869–1877
Rutherford B. Hayes, 1877–1881
James A. Garfield, 1881
Chester Arthur, 1881–1885

Grover Cleveland, 1885–1889
Benjamin Harrison, 1889–1893
Grover Cleveland, 1893–1897
William McKinley, 1897–1901
Theodore Roosevelt, 1901–1909
William H. Taft, 1909–1913
Woodrow Wilson, 1913–1921
Warren G. Harding, 1921–1923
Calvin Coolidge, 1923–1929
Herbert Hoover, 1929–1933
Franklin D. Roosevelt, 1933–1945
Harry S. Truman, 1945–1953
Dwight D. Eisenhower, 1953–1961
John F. Kennedy, 1961–1963
Lyndon B. Johnson, 1963–1969
Richard M. Nixon, 1969–1974
Gerald R. Ford, 1974–1977
Jimmy Carter, 1977–1981
Ronald Reagan, 1981–1989
George H. W. Bush, 1989–1993
William J. Clinton, 1993–2001
George W. Bush, 2001–2009
Barack Obama, 2009–

Glossary

acceptance speech — a speech a politician gives when he or she wins an election

challenge — a difficult task

election — the act of choosing someone or deciding something by voting

equal rights — something that the law says a person can do; equal rights means a person is treated the same as someone else regardless of their race, age, or gender.

improve — to make better

popular — liked by many people

vote — to make a choice in an election

Internet Sites

FactHound offers a safe, fun way to find Internet sites related to this book. All of the sites on Facthound have been researched by our staff.

Here's all you do:

Visit *www.facthound.com*

FactHound will fetch the best sites for you!

Glosario

el desafío — una tarea difícil

el discurso de aceptación — un discurso que da un político cuando él o ella gana una elección

las elecciones — el acto de elegir a alguien o decidir algo por medio del voto

la igualdad de derechos — algo que la ley dice que una persona puede hacer; igualdad de derechos significa que una persona es tratada de la misma manera que otra sin importar su raza, edad o género.

mejorar — hacer mejor

popular — estimado por mucha gente

votar — seleccionar en unas elecciones

Sitios de Internet

FactHound brinda una forma segura y divertida de encontrar sitios de Internet relacionados con este libro. Todos los sitios en FactHound han sido investigados por nuestro personal.

Esto es todo lo que tú necesitas hacer:
Visita *www.facthound.com*

¡FactHound buscará los mejores sitios para ti!

Index

Índice